Original title:
Winter's Allure

Copyright © 2024 Swan Charm
All rights reserved.

Author: Olivia Oja
ISBN HARDBACK: 978-9916-79-606-1
ISBN PAPERBACK: 978-9916-79-607-8
ISBN EBOOK: 978-9916-79-608-5

Beneath a Shimmering Blanket

Beneath a shimmering blanket,
The stars begin to glow,
Whispers of the night air,
Softly dance below.

Moonlight spills like silver,
Upon the silent land,
Dreams weave through the shadows,
With a gentle hand.

Crickets sing their sweet song,
As the trees sway in tune,
Nature blankets the world,
In the arms of the moon.

Every breath feels magic,
Every moment divine,
Under the vast canvas,
Where the sky starts to shine.

As dawn brushes the edges,
Of the night's calm retreat,
The shimmering blanket fades,
Leaving dreams at our feet.

Frosted Dreams Take Flight

Frosted dreams take flight,
On the wings of the breeze,
Whispers through the branches,
Bring the heart to ease.

A chill in the twilight,
Holds the secrets of night,
Every shadow glimmers,
In the soft, pale light.

Snowflakes swirl like dancers,
In a delicate spree,
Painting all around us,
In pure harmony.

Each step on the pathway,
Leaves a trace of delight,
As frosted dreams awaken,
In the stillness of night.

The world a quiet marvel,
A canvas of the free,
With frosted dreams taking,
Flight, endlessly.

The Embrace of Frozen Twilight

The embrace of frozen twilight,
Enfolds the weary day,
With shades of blue and silver,
In a soft ballet.

Footsteps muffled gently,
Upon the crisp white air,
Every corner whispers,
A secret hidden there.

Clouds weave tales of wonder,
As stars begin to spark,
The sky, a painted canvas,
Where shadows gently arc.

In this hushed serenade,
Time feels slow and sweet,
With the embrace of twilight,
Pulling hearts to meet.

As darkness holds the thinnest,
Of a lingering light,
We find warmth in the silence,
Of the frozen night.

Crystal Lace of Dawn

Crystal lace of dawn,
Adorns the waking trees,
Nature's art emerging,
In the softest breeze.

Gentle hues of amber,
Brush the edges of night,
As the world awakens,
To the golden light.

Every drop of dew shines,
Like jewels in the morn,
Each blade of grass glistens,
As the sun is reborn.

Birdsong fills the silence,
With harmony so sweet,
In the glow of the crystal,
Life rises to greet.

The day stretches before us,
With a promise renewed,
In the crystal lace of dawn,
Hope finds its way through.

Luminous Frostbite

In the quiet of the night,
Frost begins to glow,
Under stars' soft light,
Ice crystals dance below.

Cold breath on the air,
Whispers of wonder call,
The world wrapped in care,
Nature's sparkling thrall.

Branches cloaked in white,
A chill that feels alive,
Each flake, a pure delight,
In this frost, we thrive.

Pain of winter's kiss,
Yet beauty in the freeze,
In shadows we find bliss,
Among the frozen trees.

As dawn breaks the night,
Colors splinter and shine,
Witness the frostbite,
In this moment, divine.

Odes to the Icebound Earth

Amidst the silent freeze,
Echoes of ages past,
Nature's cobalt tease,
In ice is beauty cast.

Crags draped in snow's veil,
Mountains stand tall and proud,
Legends in the trail,
Whispers soft and loud.

The river's frozen song,
Melodies of the cold,
In this embrace, we belong,
Nature's tales unfold.

Stars twinkle like dreams,
In the depths of the night,
These frozen, fleeting beams,
Inspire hearts to fight.

Let us honor this land,
Where ice and spirit blend,
In the stillness we stand,
Odes to the earth we send.

Whispers of the Arctic Night

Underneath the pale moon,
A serenity unfolds,
In the darkened cocoon,
Magic in the cold.

Glistening fields of white,
Silent shadows creep,
In the arms of night,
The world lies asleep.

Secrets on the wind,
Cryptic tales take flight,
Nature's pulse rescinds,
Whispers of the night.

Footsteps soft and light,
Echoes that will fade,
Through the frosty sight,
In dreams we wade.

Cherish this still grace,
In the heart of the freeze,
The night's soft embrace,
In each breath, unease.

Caress of the Snowy Gale

The winds softly sigh,
As snowflakes kiss the ground,
Carrying whispers high,
In their frosty sound.

Nature's gentle breath,
Sways trees in quiet bliss,
In this dance of death,
Life's beauty we won't miss.

With each gust we feel,
A caress from the skies,
In this wintry reel,
Softness in disguise.

Frozen dreams take flight,
Waltzing on crystal beams,
Guided by the light,
Of soft, shimmering dreams.

Let us revel here,
In the chill and the grace,
The snowflakes we cheer,
In winter's warm embrace.

Tranquility in Teardrop Form

In the stillness of the night,
Soft whispers brush my skin,
Every tear a quiet thought,
A moment held within.

Moonlight dances on the ground,
Each glimmer speaks my name,
Shadows weave a gentle song,
In solitude, no shame.

Rivers flow with silent grace,
Washing sorrow's taste away,
Here, in peace, I find my place,
In teardrops, I will stay.

Every droplet, a release,
Of burdens worn too long,
In the heart, a quiet peace,
Within, I still belong.

Tranquility, my guiding star,
In darkness, hope ignites,
For every tear, a distant spark,
Reflects my endless nights.

The Sorcery of Silvered Pines

Among the towering trees so grand,
A world of whispers dwells,
Silvered branches weave their spell,
Where magic softly swells.

Beneath their boughs, secrets sleep,
In shadows deep and wide,
Each sigh of wind, a promise kept,
Ancient tales collide.

Moonlit paths call out to me,
In twilight's tender glow,
From roots to sky, enchantments weave,
In pines where cool winds blow.

With every step, I lose my way,
Yet find what's lost before,
Among the silvered, silent trees,
I seek the heart's deep core.

Magic flows in every breeze,
A sorceress's delight,
In silvered pines, my soul takes flight,
Embracing endless night.

Twilight's Numb Embrace

In twilight's soft, enfolding arms,
The world begins to fade,
Whispers of the day retreat,
In shadows, dreams are laid.

Colors melt in dusky light,
A canvas vast and bare,
Silent calls of night appear,
With mysteries to share.

Footsteps echo on the ground,
Where silence claims its right,
The hum of life now hushed and still,
In tender, cloaked night.

Embrace the numbness of the hour,
Let worries drift away,
As time stands still in this embrace,
In twilight's gentle sway.

Within this calm, I find my peace,
A moment stretched in grace,
For in the dark, I find the light,
In twilight's warm embrace.

In the Arms of Icy Shadows

In the arms of icy shadows,
Whispers of the night abide,
Echoes of the frost-laden air,
Where secrets often hide.

Cold hands reach through silken dreams,
A chill wraps round my soul,
In stillness, I confront my fears,
As darkness takes its toll.

The moon, a silent sentinel,
Watches over my plight,
In the grasp of icy shadows,
I seek the spark of light.

Shivers dance beneath my skin,
Yet warmth begins to bloom,
In fragility, I break the ice,
Defying dusk's dark tomb.

With every breath, I find my strength,
In shadows' cold embrace,
For in their arms, I grow anew,
Transforming fear to grace.

Breath of a Snowflake

A single flake drifts down,
Whispers soft upon the ground.
Each one holds a tale untold,
In its dance, the world unfolds.

Gentle touch of winter's breath,
A fleeting moment, life and death.
In crystal patterns soft and bright,
They shimmer softly in the light.

Frosted lace on window panes,
Nature's art through cold terrains.
Each flake's grace a fragile gift,
Silent beauty, hearts they lift.

When they gather, silent, white,
A blanket soft in the night.
Cloaked in wonder, still, serene,
A world transformed, a dream unseen.

As daylight fades, they gently fade,
A memory of the dance they've made.
Breath of a snowflake, pure and free,
A moment caught in tranquility.

Frosted Serenade

Underneath the silver moon,
Frost has wrapped the world in tune.
Silent nights with stars aglow,
Nature's voice, a soft, sweet flow.

Branches draped in icy lace,
Each glimmer holds a fleeting grace.
In the hush, the whispers rise,
To swell beneath the winter skies.

Footsteps crunch on frozen trails,
Echoes of the chill that hails.
Every sound, a muted note,
In the stillness, seasons float.

Harmonies of the winter night,
Twinkling dreams in soft twilight.
Awakened hearts to nature's song,
In frost's embrace, we all belong.

Frosted serenade, so dear,
Winter's magic, crystal clear.
As the night unfolds its breath,
A fragile dance, a hint of death.

A Symphony of Falling Feathers

Feathers fall like softest rain,
Twirling softly, joy and pain.
In the hush of winter's dome,
Each one finds a place, a home.

Whispers weave through the cool air,
Silence cloaked in beauty rare.
Dancing gently, wild and free,
Nature's touch in white debris.

A symphony, the heart does sing,
Every flake, a sacred thing.
In their journey, life interweaves,
With each landing, hope believes.

Layers deep, a quilt of white,
Holding warmth in starry night.
Snowflakes twirl, a tale retold,
In their beauty, secrets hold.

A final bow, they grace the ground,
In their essence, peace is found.
A symphony of falling shades,
In winter's arms, the world cascades.

Whispers Beneath the Snow

In the silence, below the white,
Echoes linger, dreams take flight.
Whispers soft, beneath the frost,
Memory's warmth, never lost.

Each flake carries a story deep,
In their stillness, hearts will keep.
A world wrapped in a shroud of peace,
In winter's hug, our cares release.

Crystalline secrets gently weave,
Tales of beauty, we believe.
Every layer hides a spark,
A promise sleeping in the dark.

Gentle sighs as winter sings,
Life beneath the snow, it clings.
Awake in slumber, waiting still,
Hope and wonder, heartbeats fill.

Whispers beneath, in shadows cast,
Hints of spring, the seasons' fast.
As silence reigns, beneath the glow,
Dreams take form in whispers low.

Silence Wrapped in White

Snowflakes fall softly, like whispers of night,
Blankets of silence cover the earth quite.
Footprints are lost in the shimmering gleam,
Nature holds still, wrapped in a dream.

Trees wear their coats made of winter's delight,
Branches adorned, sparkling, icy and bright.
A hush in the air speaks secrets untold,
Silence wraps all in its quiet enfold.

The moon casts its glow on this tranquil scene,
Awakening magic in shadows unseen.
Each breath we take mingles with frosted air,
In silence we find peace beyond all compare.

Crystalline Reveries

In the stillness, dreams sail on crystalline lakes,
Mirrors reflecting the magic that wakes.
Frosted petals, delicate, bloom at dawn,
Whispers of beauty softly withdrawn.

Gentle winds carry secrets from afar,
Each icy breath draws us closer to stars.
Moments suspended in shimmering lights,
Crystalline reveries dance through the nights.

Nature's pure canvas, painted in white,
Every contour aglow in the moon's light.
As echoes of silence stretch wide and profound,
In dreams we wander where wonders abound.

The Magic of Moonglow

Under the cloak of a velvet night sky,
Moonglow enchants, as the world whispers by.
Silver beams wrap around each hidden place,
Casting a spell of serene, tender grace.

Shadows entwine, making patterns that sway,
While stars wink in tunes of an ancient ballet.
The heart feels a stir, as if time holds its breath,
In the magic of moonglow, we find life and death.

Secrets of night perch on the horizon,
Embers of dreams, like thoughts in a prison.
With each gentle sigh, the night softly glows,
In this tranquil embrace, our wonder still grows.

Dance of the Winter Stars

Through the cold, clear night, the winter stars play,
Twinkling and glowing, they light up the way.
A dance in the sky, they shimmer and swirl,
Guiding lost hearts in a cosmic unfurl.

Wrapped in the darkness, they sing of the bold,
Stories of ages in silence retold.
Under their gaze, the world feels so small,
Yet in their embrace, we find strength for all.

The chill in the air breathes life into dreams,
As stardust and wishes flow down like soft streams.
In the dance of the winter stars, we refrain,
Finding warmth in the echoes of joy and of pain.

Veil of Frosted Dreams

In the morning's gentle light,
Frosty whispers take their flight.
Shimmering trails on fields of white,
Nature winks, a sweet delight.

Beneath a sky so vast and blue,
A tapestry of dreams anew.
With every breath, the world feels bright,
Veils of magic, pure and true.

Silhouettes of trees stand tall,
Crystals formed from winter's call.
In this realm, we feel the thrall,
As winter blankets over all.

Frozen lakes like mirrors gleam,
Echoing our quiet dream.
Moments drift like softest steam,
In the heart of winter's theme.

With each step, a crunching sound,
A symphony, profound, unbound.
Veil of frost, our souls are crowned,
In nature's spell, we're tightly wound.

Mysteries in the Glacial Glow

Amidst the shadows, secrets stir,
Beneath the ice, the whispers blur.
Glacial glow, dreams do confer,
In the stillness, hearts occur.

Twinkling stars like scattered gems,
Lighting paths like ancient hymns.
In frozen realms where silence hems,
Lost stories breathe in soft diadems.

Crystals dance in moonlit streams,
In their depths, the night redeems.
Mysteries carried on the beams,
A world alive with silver dreams.

Echoes linger, soft and low,
Each breath a secret to bestow.
In the cold, our spirits grow,
Bound together in the flow.

Winding paths through icy trees,
Nature's breath, an endless tease.
In glacial glow, the heart's at ease,
Holding close the winter breeze.

Quietude Wrapped in White

Softly blankets cover ground,
In white silence, peace is found.
Nature hums a soothing sound,
Wrapped in quiet, dreams abound.

Snowflakes dance in soft embrace,
Delicate and full of grace.
Every flake a silent trace,
Of winter's love, a soft face.

Huddled close, the creatures dwell,
In their warmth, a winter's spell.
Nature weaves a timeless shell,
In quietude, all is well.

Frosted branches glimmer bright,
Underneath the pale moonlight.
In the stillness of the night,
Wrapped in calm, we hold on tight.

With every breath, the world slows down,
In this wonderland, no frown.
Quietude wraps, a gentle gown,
A snowy peace in the town.

Frozen Dreams Under Starlight

Underneath the night's embrace,
Starlit whispers fill the space.
Frozen dreams in tender lace,
A symphony of time and place.

Glistening crowns on snowflakes ride,
Cascading down in nature's stride.
We hold our breath, the world beside,
In this moment, hearts collide.

Whispers of the cosmos call,
In frozen realms, we find our all.
Stars above, a shimmering wall,
Knitting dreams both great and small.

Clouds drift softly, shadows blend,
Wandering thoughts that never end.
In winter's arms, we shall amend,
As frozen dreams around us tend.

Embers of hope in twilight's blink,
In the chill, our spirits link.
Under starlight, we softly think,
In frozen dreams, we dive and sink.

Lanterns in the Frost

Frosted lanterns glow with light,
Whispers dance in the cold night air,
Shadows flicker, take their flight,
Silent secrets everywhere.

Underneath the starry skies,
Branches glisten, silver bright,
Every echo softly sighs,
Wrapped in warmth of winter's night.

Footprints crunch on icy ground,
Tales of journeys left behind,
In the stillness, hope is found,
Kindled dreams by lanterns bind.

Around the hearth, stories blend,
Voices rise with gentle grace,
While outside, the cold winds send,
Magic stirs in every space.

Frosted paths weave through the trees,
Guiding hearts where shadows play,
In this realm, the spirit frees,
Carried forth on winter's sway.

Snow-dusted Reveries

Softly falls the purest snow,
Blanketing the world so wide,
Dreams awaken, pulses grow,
In this calm, the heart can glide.

Whispers from the snowy pines,
Crystals catch the waning light,
Every moment intertwines,
In the hush of gentle night.

Footsteps lead to paths unknown,
Adventures spark in frosty air,
In this vastness, spirit's grown,
Chasing wonders everywhere.

Laughter echoes, children play,
Snowflakes twirl in joyful flight,
Here together, dreams won't stray,
Wrapped in warmth of pure delight.

As the evening starts to glow,
Moonlight dances on the scene,
In the quiet, sweet and slow,
Snow-dusted dreams weave through the serene.

Frozen Pathways of Thought

In the stillness, silence reigns,
Frozen pathways softly gleam,
Thoughts like snowflakes fall like rain,
Captured in a fleeting dream.

Through the woods, where shadows sleep,
Mind's reflections weave and bend,
Crystalline the secrets keep,
On these paths, the soul can mend.

Every step a story told,
Every breath a frozen sigh,
In the beauty, hearts grow bold,
Searching for the reason why.

Frosted whispers draw us near,
To the places long hidden,
Here in wonder, there is cheer,
A journey's end never bidden.

With each moment, visions blend,
In the chill, a warmth ignites,
Frozen pathways do not end,
They lead to the starry nights.

The Solace of Falling Snow

Snow descends in soft embrace,
Covering the world so white,
Each flake dances with such grace,
In the silence of the night.

Cozy fires glow from within,
Hearts alight with warmth and cheer,
Outside, nature's hush begins,
In this peace, there's nothing to fear.

Thoughts like snowflakes spin and twirl,
Drifting down from skies above,
In their fall, the mind unfurls,
Wrapped in winter's gentle love.

Candlelight through frosted glass,
Glimmers in the evening pale,
In this moment, time will pass,
And serenity prevails.

As the night wraps all in white,
Every tree adorned with glow,
Find the solace in this sight,
In the beauty of falling snow.

The Art of Icy Beauty

In the dawn's gentle grace,
Shimmering crystals take place.
Snowflakes dance with delight,
Nature's art in pure white.

Branches wear a glistening crown,
Silent whispers of the town.
Each flake tells a story soft,
In the chill, spirits lift aloft.

Frosted windows, a world inside,
Where dreams and memories abide.
A canvas of winter so bright,
Captures hearts in the night.

Ice laces the landscape near,
Jewel-toned and crystal clear.
Beneath the chill, warmth resides,
In the beauty that winter hides.

At dusk, the sky turns to grey,
Yet the beauty's here to stay.
In the stillness, art unfolds,
A chilly tale that never grows old.

Chiaroscuro of the Season

In shadows deep, the light does play,
Soft hues of night blend with day.
Beneath the branches, secrets lie,
As twilight whispers a soft sigh.

The trees stand tall in dark and light,
Their silhouettes a stunning sight.
Frosty breaths of winter chill,
Contrast with warmth, a gentle thrill.

Golden rays melt the pristine white,
A canvas brushed, from dark to bright.
Colors shift in the fading sun,
A dance of tones, a battle won.

Silent streets wear a shadowy coat,
Echoes of laughter, conversations float.
In the evening's embrace, life finds a way,
A chiaroscuro in shades of grey.

Each moment, a flicker, a fleeting spark,
In winter's hold, life leaves its mark.
Nature's play of light and shade,
Crafts a masterpiece, never to fade.

Threads of Snowy Veil

A veil descends, soft and slow,
Weaving secrets in its glow.
Silent threads touch earth and sky,
Transformation, a whispered sigh.

Delicate lace on every pine,
Each flake a story, intertwine.
Winds weave patterns, wild and free,
A tapestry of harmony.

In the quiet, echoes ring,
Nature's lullaby to sing.
Frozen dreams buried deep below,
In a world wrapped in snowy glow.

Gentle folds embrace the night,
Crystals glimmer, pure and bright.
A snowy shroud, soft and deep,
In winter's arms, the earth does sleep.

Underneath, life waits to bloom,
Ready to shed the cold's costume.
Threads of snow, a fleeting grace,
A promise of warmth in a cold embrace.

Frosty Footprints of Time

Footprints pressed in the glistening snow,
Tell the tales of where we go.
Each step marks a moment clear,
In winter's chill, we hold dear.

Whispers of winds blend with the past,
Memories, shadows, forever cast.
In the frosty air, echoes remain,
Stories linger, joy and pain.

Lost in wanderings, hearts entwined,
Nature's lens, so unconfined.
Snowflakes fall, a fleeting chance,
Time stands still in this quiet dance.

With every chill, a warmth inside,
Awakens dreams we try to hide.
Frosty footprints lead the way,
Guiding us through night and day.

In the depths of winter's embrace,
Footprints fade but leave a trace.
A journey penned on a frozen line,
In the land where moments shine.

Tales Written in Crystal

In the morning light, they gleam,
Stories held in every beam.
Whispers of the past unfold,
In crystal tales, their glories told.

Each drop a moment, pure and clear,
Reflecting dreams we hold so dear.
The world transformed by nature's hand,
In silence, on the sparkling land.

Time's gentle flow, a shimmering stream,
Carving paths through winter's dream.
Nature's voice in icy hues,
A canvas painted, cold as blues.

Beneath the sky, so vast, so wide,
Crystal worlds where secrets bide.
In every shard a glimpse of fate,
Of lives entwined, so intricate.

As sunlight fades, the stories change,
In twilight's grasp, the hues arrange.
With every gleam, a soul set free,
In crystal tales, our memories.

The Lullaby of Snowflakes

Softly falling from the sky,
Gentle whispers, drifting by.
Each flake a dream, unique, untold,
A lullaby wrapped in purest cold.

Dancing down like fleeting sighs,
In the twilight, as day dies.
Covering earth in a quilt so white,
Cradling the world in softest light.

Children laugh as they swirl around,
Voices echo, pure joy found.
In the silence, a magical sound,
The lullaby of joy unbound.

Night's embrace begins to creep,
As snowflakes settle, drift and sleep.
In the stillness, hearts ignite,
With dreams unfolding, pure and bright.

Each flake a wish, a secret dream,
Wonder carried on a frozen stream.
In winter's arms, we find our peace,
The lullaby of snowflakes, sweet release.

Glistening Tapestries of The Night

Stars above in velvet skies,
Weaving tales as darkness flies.
Threads of silver, woven tight,
Glistening tapestries of the night.

Moonbeams spill on quiet seas,
Dancing shadows, soft night breeze.
Each twinkle holds a secret place,
Patterns glowing in timeless grace.

Whispers travel on the wind,
Stories of the stars rescind.
In the heart of night, we find,
Dreams and hopes intricately twined.

A symphony of distant light,
Illuminating our shared plight.
In every stitch, a story spun,
Of all we've lost and all that's won.

As dawn approaches, colors fade,
Yet the memories never evade.
In every night, a chance to soar,
A tapestry we can't ignore.

Moonlit Whispers on the Frost

Moonlight dances on the frost,
Silent whispers, a world embossed.
Each shimmer holds a secret still,
As night beckons, with a chill.

Trees wear crowns of icy lace,
Enchanted by the moon's embrace.
In every glint, a tale unfolds,
Of mysteries that the night holds.

Footprints crunched beneath our feet,
Echoes of the night, so sweet.
In the hush, our breaths combine,
As moonlit whispers intertwine.

Stars gaze down with watchful eyes,
Guardians of our lowly cries.
In their glow, we find our way,
Through the magic of the gray.

With dawn's approach, the whispers fade,
Yet in our hearts, they are replayed.
Moonlit nights, forever lost,
In the dance of frost, we're embossed.

Snow-Laden Solitudes

In quiet woods, the snowflakes fall,
Whispers of winter, a gentle call.
Blanketing earth in a shroud of white,
Silent dreams dance in the night.

Footprints trace paths, where few have tread,
Nature's cocoon, a soft, warm bed.
Each flake unique, a fleeting grace,
Time seems to pause in this tranquil space.

The world feels slow, yet still it breathes,
Under the weight of winter's wreaths.
Above, the stars twinkle, crisp and clear,
Guiding the hearts that wander near.

Branches bow low, heavy with snow,
A landscape transformed, a mystical show.
Stillness reigns, as dreams take flight,
In snow-laden solitudes, pure delight.

An Elegy in Flurries

A mournful sigh in the chilly air,
As flurries drift, beyond compare.
The trees stand bare, in solemn grace,
Nature weeps in this frozen space.

Each flake a tear, soft and light,
Echoes of loves lost in the night.
Whispers of warmth once held tight,
Now fading dreams in the autumn's plight.

The horizon dull, the sun concealed,
In winter's grasp, our fates are sealed.
Yet hope remains in the falling white,
A promise of spring, beyond the night.

Through shadows cast by frosted limbs,
Life clings on, as winter dims.
In these flurries, a tale unfolds,
Of love's embrace, and memories cold.

Captive by the Cold

In frosty grips, the world does sigh,
Captive by the cold, beneath grey sky.
The breath of winter, sharp and keen,
Wraps the earth in a crystal sheen.

Days are muted, shadows blend,
Frozen whispers from trees extend.
Children's laughter, echoes near,
Amid the chill, warmth draws us near.

Crisp air bites, while fires ignite,
As evening falls, we hold our light.
Cocoa warms hands, with stories shared,
In every heart, love is declared.

Each fleeting moment, a treasure stored,
As winter's canvas is deftly poured.
Nature sleeps, but dreams reside,
In the heart of those, winter's glide.

Pines Cloaked in Frost

Tall pines stand, cloaked in frost,
In this wonderland, never lost.
Needles glisten in the pale light,
Guardians of day, sentinels of night.

Silence wraps around their form,
A tranquil peace, the hush before a storm.
Footfalls muted, beneath soft snow,
Through stories told, the old winds blow.

Boughs heavy, bowed with grace,
Nature's touch on this sacred space.
A tapestry woven with winter's breath,
In pines that stand, defying death.

Beneath their shade, dreams take flight,
In this realm of crisp delight.
Together we gather, hearts entwined,
In pines cloaked in frost, solace we find.

Beneath the Crystal Canopy

In the woods, beneath the trees,
A glimmering world, soft as a breeze.
Branches adorned with diamonds' rays,
Whispering secrets of sunlit days.

The shadows dance in dappled light,
Nature's canvas, a wondrous sight.
Birds sing sweetly in morning's glow,
While gentle streams hum tales below.

Leaves murmur tales of hidden dreams,
Where every sparkle brightly beams.
In this realm, all worries cease,
Beneath the canopy, find your peace.

Time ebbs away, lost in embrace,
Here, moments linger, slow their pace.
With whispers soft as twilight's sigh,
Beneath the sky, we learn to fly.

Each heartbeat echoes through the green,
In nature's arms, we feel serene.
So take a breath, let worries fade,
Beneath the canopy, joy is made.

A Serenade of Snow

Flakes fall gently, pure and white,
Blanketing the world, a wondrous sight.
In silence wrapped, the earth does rest,
Winter's song, nature's best.

Footprints trace a path anew,
Every step a dance in view.
Children laugh in frosty air,
Building dreams with joyful flair.

Whispers of the cold wind's kiss,
A tranquil moment, pure bliss.
Hills adorned in crystal haze,
Fleeting memories of sunny days.

Night descends, stars gleam so bright,
Moonlight dances, casting light.
In this stillness, hearts align,
A serenade, sweet and divine.

As dawn awakens, the world will glow,
Nature sighs in the fresh, soft snow.
In every drift, a tale is spun,
A winter's song, forever begun.

Breath of the Frozen Air

Crisp and clear, the morning breaks,
While icy winds, the silence shakes.
Each breath visible, a fleeting dream,
In winter's grasp, all hopes redeem.

Frosted pines stand tall and proud,
Guardians of the winter shroud.
Whispers echo through the trees,
Carried gently on the freeze.

A moment still, where time stands still,
Nature's pulse, a steady thrill.
Every heartbeat matches the flow,
In the breath of the frozen, we grow.

Ice crystals shimmer in pale light,
Creating miracles in plain sight.
Through every chill, we learn to feel,
In cold embrace, our hearts can heal.

So take a moment, breathe it in,
Let winter's magic, warmth begin.
In frozen air, connections bloom,
In every sigh, dispelling gloom.

The Lure of the Stillness

In quiet moments, shadows play,
The world retreats, softens the fray.
With each heartbeat, the silence calls,
A gentle echo through the halls.

Time drips slowly, like honey sweet,
In tranquil spaces, we find our seat.
Thoughts meander, easy and free,
In the stillness, we start to see.

Nature holds her breath, so pure,
Moments of peace, a sacred cure.
Whispers of leaves, a soft lament,
In stillness, our souls are content.

The lure of calm wraps like a shawl,
A refuge found where worries fall.
In silence deep, we learn to rest,
In stillness' arms, we are our best.

Let echoes linger, soft and bright,
In the stillness, holds delight.
So pause awhile, let your heart swim,
In quiet realms, the light won't dim.

Glistening Silence

In the hush of night, stars gleam bright,
Whispers of the moon, a soft, pure light.
Snowflakes dance down, a gentle sigh,
Wrapped in this peace, the world stands by.

Footprints lost in a blanket white,
Nature's embrace, a tranquil sight.
Crystals adorn every branch and leaf,
In this stillness, I find relief.

Voices fade into a velvet shroud,
Secrets held in silence, proud.
Echoes of dreams float through the air,
Glistening moments, beyond compare.

The heartbeat of the night, so calm,
A soothing balm, a sacred psalm.
Each breath a treasure, crisp and clear,
In this sacred silence, I feel you near.

As dawn approaches, colors ignite,
A symphony of warmth, chasing night.
Yet in the glistening, stillness stays,
A cherished memory of tranquil days.

Hibernal Dreams

Beneath the quilt of frosted white,
Nature sleeps in the depth of night.
Whispers of warmth in the cold air,
Hibernal dreams, a peaceful lair.

Animals nestled in their snug burrows,
While the world above is swept in sorrows.
Time slows down in this serene space,
As visions dance with gentle grace.

Stars twinkle softly in the sky,
Guiding the dreams that float on high.
Fleeting images of sunlit days,
Amidst the chill, a longing phrase.

Each sigh of wind tells tales untold,
Of hidden wonders in the bold.
In the stillness, a promise gleams,
Awakening hearts from their hibernal dreams.

As winter wanes, the earth will stir,
Life will return, a joyful blur.
But in this moment, we're held tight,
In hibernal dreams, lost to the night.

Shadows of the Frost

Beneath the guise of winter's breath,
Lay shadows cast by life and death.
Silhouettes of trees, stark and bare,
In the frosty glow, a haunting air.

Footfalls echo on the icy ground,
Whispers carried, a haunting sound.
Moments captured in glistening ice,
Reflections of seasons, a quiet slice.

Bright stars shimmer in the deep blue,
Chasing away shadows, night anew.
Yet in their glow, still hints of dark,
Frosted secrets, a lingering spark.

Nature listens, holds her breath tight,
Cradling dreams through the long night.
Each shadow whispers, in hushed tones,
Stories of frost, of life, of bones.

In the dawn's embrace, shadows recede,
Yet their essence lingers, hearts they feed.
For in the frost, both light and shade,
Dance together, a bond well-made.

Midnight's Chill

The clock strikes twelve, a moment still,
Awash in shadows, the night's cold thrill.
A breath of frost upon the pane,
Midnight whispers, a soft refrain.

Stars twinkle brightly, way up high,
Glimmers of warmth in the vaulted sky.
Yet below, the world is hushed and tight,
Wrapped in the cloak of the endless night.

The moon spills silver on the ground,
Casting its hue, a shimmering sound.
Crickets serenade with soft, sweet tunes,
Midnight's wanderer, beneath the moons.

Sleepy towns, all draped in white,
Cuddled dreams, lost in the night.
Each heart beats slowly, time seems to pause,
Held in the chill, wrapped without cause.

But in this quiet, awaken the soul,
With midnight's chill, we feel whole.
For in the dark, the world finds light,
Embraced by the magic of a starry night.

Glacial Lullabies

Whispers of ice in the still of night,
Moonlight dances, casting silver light.
Beneath the surface, the secrets lie,
Nature's heartbeat, a gentle sigh.

Cold winds carry a soft refrain,
Melodies etched in the frozen plain.
Crystals shimmer, a timeless song,
In glacial arms, we all belong.

Heartbeat of the Snow

Amidst the silence, a soft pulse grows,
Each flake falls gently, like whispered prose.
Underneath layers, life starts to form,
Nature's breath, a soothing storm.

Frozen branches sway with grace,
Memories linger in this sacred space.
Every drift tells a story deep,
Awakening dreams from winter's sleep.

Veils of Frosted Light

A tapestry woven with threads of ice,
Glowing softly, so pure and nice.
Wrapped in brilliance, the world does shine,
Each glint a promise, each spark a sign.

Morning awakens, the frost may fade,
Yet in the heart, these dreams are laid.
Veils of enchantment, a fleeting glance,
In chilly silence, our spirits dance.

Shimmering Shadows

In twilight's embrace, the shadows play,
Flickering whispers at the end of day.
Glistening edges, a dance of frost,
Moments gleam, though they may be lost.

Echoes of stillness, secrets unfold,
Tales of the night in darkness told.
With every twinkle, a memory stays,
In shimmering shadows, we find our days.

Glimpse of a Hibernating Heart

In the depths where silence dwells,
Winter breathes in whispered spells.
A heartbeat slows, wrapped tight in dreams,
Among the frost where stillness beams.

Time passes slow, a tranquil hold,
The secrets of the night unfold.
A faint pulse stirs beneath the ice,
Yearning for warmth, a hint of spice.

Hidden deep, the spirit sleeps,
Cradled in the quiet leaps.
Awakening soon, with a gentle sigh,
Underneath the vast, cold sky.

Whispers of spring, a distant call,
Yet here in silence, the heart stands tall.
Roots spread wide, grounded in peace,
In this hibernation, fears release.

Oh, to behold what's yet to be,
Emerging from winter's quiet plea.
A glimpse of life, a dance of light,
As the heart prepares to take flight.

Enchanted by the Cold

A crystal world, where dreams are spun,
Underneath the pale, bright sun.
Frosted branches, a charming sight,
Whispers of magic in the night.

Footprints trace where few have tread,
Enchanted paths, where hearts are led.
Shimmering stars above us glow,
In the dance of frost, we ebb and flow.

The chill wraps round like a lover's grasp,
In icy hands, our joys we clasp.
Each breath a cloud, a tale retold,
In this frozen realm, we're bold.

Snowflakes twirl in a graceful waltz,
Nature's rhythm, no faults.
A serenade of winter's breath,
A fleeting glimpse of life and death.

Enchanted hearts amidst the chill,
In the silence, time stands still.
We dance, we dream, till warmth returns,
In frozen wonder, the heart still burns.

Frostbitten Fantasies

Beneath the frost, dreams intertwined,
Whispers of longing, gently aligned.
Each flake a story, a wish held tight,
In the hush of the cold, lost in the night.

Frozen petals, colors fade,
Yet in stillness, memories laid.
The chill bites deep, a sweet despair,
In the frostbitten moonlight, love lays bare.

Dreams take flight on icy wings,
Through the silence, the heart still sings.
Fantasies bloom in the quiet glow,
In this winter's heart, seeds we sow.

Each breath a fog, a moment's glee,
Frostbitten visions, wild and free.
Lost in the magic of the frozen air,
Life's gentle touch, a love laid bare.

Yet as the thaw begins to stir,
The heart's lost wishes softly blur.
What was once frozen now starts to flow,
From frostbitten fantasies, warmth will grow.

A Legacy of Frozen Breath

In the air, a legacy breathes,
Carried forth on winter's wreath.
A tapestry woven with silent strands,
In the frost lies life's gentle hands.

The beauty of stillness, a wise refrain,
Echoes of laughter from autumn's pain.
With each exhale, a story unveiled,
Upon the landscape, where dreams have sailed.

We walk this path of glittering white,
Hand in hand through the freezing night.
Memories etched in the icy glow,
A legacy where love shall flow.

Each breath we take, a note in time,
A winter's tale, a whispered rhyme.
Through the frost, our spirits sing,
A legacy of love that winter brings.

Together we face the coming thaw,
In the warmth, we find our awe.
From frozen breath, new life shall bloom,
Through winter's grasp, we find our room.

Sleds and Soft Shadows

The children laugh on hills so high,
Sleds racing fast beneath the sky.
Soft shadows play on the shimmering snow,
Winter's embrace, a gentle glow.

Tracks left behind tell stories old,
Of laughter shared in the winter's cold.
Bright cheeks flushed in the frosty air,
Memories made, moments rare.

Mittens and scarves, colors so bright,
Against the white, a pure delight.
As twilight falls, the snowflakes gleam,
In the fading light, a child's dream.

The moon rises high, a silvery friend,
As the evening trails begin to blend.
Sleds resting now, by fireside warm,
Wrapped in stories, away from harm.

Soft shadows linger, whispers of play,
In the hearts of children, forever stay.
Through winters passed, and those to come,
The joy of sledding will always hum.

Serene Stillness Beneath the Stars

In the quiet night, where whispers fade,
Under the sky, a vast cascade.
Stars dance softly with glowing light,
Holding secrets of the night.

Cool breezes sigh through ancient trees,
Carrying tales on the gentle breeze.
Moonlight reflects on the tranquil lake,
A mirror of dreams, still and opaque.

Fireflies flicker, a magical show,
Painting the darkness with their glow.
Each twinkling spark like a distant sun,
In the stillness, our thoughts can run.

Peace envelops as shadows creep,
Inviting the world to softly sleep.
Moments linger, timeless and pure,
In the night's embrace, we find our cure.

Beneath this dome, we feel so small,
Yet connected to it, we stand tall.
With every heartbeat, we find our place,
In the serene stillness, a gentle grace.

The Dance of Distant Lights

Across the horizon, colors collide,
In a waltz of hues, they twirl and glide.
Distant lights flicker, a vibrant spree,
Painting the canvas of night's decree.

The stars and planets, in formation they sway,
Guided by rhythms in a cosmic ballet.
Whispers of galaxies call from afar,
As dreams awaken and hopes raise the bar.

In the velvet sky, the constellations play,
Storytellers of yore, night's great display.
Each point of light, a tale to unfold,
Of love and loss, and adventures bold.

The moonbeams dance on the ocean's tide,
As waves replicate the celestial glide.
With every sparkle, the night takes a chance,
In the dance of distant lights, we prance.

So let us marvel beneath the expanse,
In the heartbeat of night, join the dance.
For every wish on a shooting star,
Brings us closer to who we are.

Shivering Sunsets

As daylight fades to a whispering glow,
The horizon blushes, a fiery show.
Crimson and gold in a passionate fight,
Embracing the dusk with all of their might.

Waves of color stretch far and wide,
Lapping at the shores with the evening tide.
The sun bows low, a tender farewell,
With secrets to keep and stories to tell.

Chill in the air, as night takes its turn,
Embers of warmth in our hearts still burn.
Birds retreat to nests, soft coos fill the air,
In the cooling evening, we linger and stare.

Each sunset shivers, a reminder so clear,
Of beauty that fades but always draws near.
In each parting light, hope finds a way,
To rise with the dawn of a brighter day.

So let us cherish these moments we find,
In shivering sunsets, we unwind.
For every end holds a promise in sight,
Of new beginnings kissed by the light.

Frosted Whispers

In the hush of winter's breath,
Whispers of frost take their flight.
Silently painting the ground,
A tapestry woven in white.

Trees wear coats of glistening silk,
While shadows stretch long in the glow.
Nature holds its secrets tight,
Beneath a blanket of snow.

Crystals dangle from branches,
Like diamonds caught in a dream.
Each flake tells a story unheard,
In the stillness, they gleam.

A cascade of whispers unfolds,
As the night wraps the world tight.
In this moment, frozen in time,
All is tranquil, all is right.

Frosted whispers softly sing,
Of the beauty in the freeze.
Nature's art, a quiet charm,
In winter's gentle breeze.

Chilling Embrace

Moonlight bathes the frozen lake,
A shimmering path of ice.
Each step forward, a chilling choice,
With nature's breath so precise.

The air is sharp, a biting kiss,
Inviting all to pause and feel.
Underneath the starry cloak,
A world so still, so surreal.

Branches arch like frozen arms,
Catching flakes that freely fall.
Wrapped in winter's chill embrace,
The silence enchants us all.

Crackling sounds beneath our feet,
Echoes whisper soft and low.
Drawing us closer to the light,
As winter's magic starts to glow.

In this moment, hearts align,
With the beauty in the cold.
A chilling embrace, serene and bright,
A story of winter, timeless and bold.

Echoes of Ice

In the stillness, echoes resound,
From deep within the icy ground.
Whispers of cold beneath the snow,
Tell tales of seasons long ago.

The crack of ice beneath our feet,
A symphony where silence meets.
Frigid air holds the sound anew,
As winter's breath leads us through.

Frosted trees stand tall and proud,
Enshrined within a crystal shroud.
Each branch a note, each leaf a tone,
In the orchestra of the cold.

Night descends, a deeper shade,
While icy echoes start to fade.
Yet still they linger, soft and clear,
Calling softly, drawing near.

In the heart of winter's chill,
Echoes of ice forever will,
Guide us through this frosty tale,
As nature's beauty will prevail.

The Silken Dance of Snowflakes

A gentle waltz from clouds above,
Snowflakes twirl in soft embrace.
Each unique, a work of art,
In the cold, they leave their trace.

Whirling softly through the air,
A silken dance, serene and light.
Falling freely, without care,
In the hush, they greet the night.

Lands transform with every flake,
Fields shimmering like dreams reborn.
The world awash in purest white,
A canvas that the storm has worn.

Children laugh as they collide,
In playful joy, they try to catch.
The fleeting grace of winter's gift,
In each moment, love is matched.

As the day turns into night,
The dance continues, pure and bright.
In the silence, snowflakes fall,
A timeless waltz, enchanting all.

Serene Slumber of the Earth

The earth lies still in gentle grace,
Wrapped in dreams, a warm embrace.
Whispers of night, soft and low,
Cradled beneath the silver glow.

Stars twinkle in the velvet sky,
While crickets sing their lullabies.
Mountains sigh with peaceful might,
Cradled in the arms of night.

The rivers hum a quiet tune,
Reflecting shadows of the moon.
Fields of grass sway in the breeze,
A symphony of tranquil peace.

Dreams unfold with every breath,
In the cradle, life and death.
The earth's heart beats in rhythmic flow,
In the serene slumber below.

Morning waits with golden hue,
To kiss the night in vibrant blue.
And as the dawn begins to rise,
The earth awakens, softly sighs.

Melodies of the Frosted World

In a world where silence reigns,
Frosty whispers, soft refrains.
Nature's breath, a crystal tune,
Awakens dreams beneath the moon.

Bare branches draped in winter's lace,
Time stands still in this frozen space.
Each flake dances, a fleeting sigh,
As gentle winds and shadows fly.

Frozen lakes reflect the light,
Glistening gems in the heart of night.
Soft crunching steps on icy ground,
In this magic, solace is found.

The air is sharp, yet crisp and clear,
Melodies of winter, pure and dear.
Each moment paused in frosted air,
Beckoning hearts with gentle care.

In this wonderland, I lose my way,
Chasing echoes of snowflakes' play.
The world transforms in a shimmering hue,
Melodies born from the silence too.

Frost-kissed Whispers

Frost-kissed mornings greet the dawn,
As nature's hush begins to yawn.
Silver blankets, soft and bright,
Wrap the earth in warmth despite the night.

Whispers drift on the chilly breeze,
Sharing secrets among the trees.
Footfalls quiet on the snow,
In the stillness, time moves slow.

The sun ascends with a tender glow,
Painting landscapes in gentle flow.
Each branch adorned with icy lace,
Captures moments in frozen space.

Voices of winter rise and fall,
Echoing softly, a haunting call.
In every flake, a story told,
Of ancient dreams and visions bold.

As evening drapes her velvet gown,
Stars emerge in a glittering crown.
Frost-kissed whispers, soft and low,
Embrace the night as shadows grow.

Silent Veils of Snow

Silent veils of snow unfold,
A tapestry of white and gold.
Each flake a whisper, soft and light,
Blanketing earth in pure delight.

Underneath the frosty sky,
Dreams of warmth and joy fly high.
Footprints trace a winding path,
In this magic, nature's wrath.

Glistening trees in icy gowns,
Shimmering jewels in winter towns.
Time stands still in the quiet air,
Wrapped in beauty, beyond compare.

Crimson sunsets bleed into night,
Painting the world in fading light.
The moon ascends, a watchful eye,
As stars emerge, lit up the sky.

In the stillness, hearts find peace,
In snowy layers, worries cease.
Silent veils embrace the ground,
In winter's arms, serenity found.

The Cloak of Chilling Starfields

A blanket of night, so vast and deep,
Whispers of secrets, the stars do keep.
Galaxies twirl in the frosty air,
Wrapped in the silence, a cosmic affair.

Winds carry tales from the void above,
Illuminated dreams, a tale of love.
Constellations dance on the edge of time,
Painting the skies with rhythms sublime.

Shadowed paths where the starlight glows,
Echoes of wonder, where no one knows.
Each twinkle a story, each spark a sigh,
Beneath the cloak, the universe lies.

In this vast sea where serenity reigns,
Infinite colors connect our veins.
We sail through the night on whispers of grace,
The cloak of chilling starfields—a sacred space.

Here, dreams take flight on soft silver beams,
And hope is reborn, like shimmering dreams.
Close your eyes, and let the night unfurl,
Wrapped in the wonders of the starlit swirl.

Canvas of Crystalline Charm

In the heart of winter, where silence sings,
A canvas unfolds with delicate wings.
Crystalline beauty spreads far and wide,
Nature's own treasure, a magical guide.

Each snowflake dances, a unique ballet,
Painting the world in a frosty display.
Sunlight reflects on the glistening white,
Transforming the morning into pure delight.

Branches wear diamonds that shimmer and glow,
Beneath icy heavens, the soft breezes blow.
Footprints remind us of the warmth we've shared,
While the canvas beckons, enchantingly bared.

A moment of stillness when time appears slow,
Wrapped in the charm of the sparkling snow.
Every breath whispers in cold, crisp air,
In this wondrous realm, we find solace rare.

A world illuminated, where magic takes flight,
In the delicate dance of day and night.
Let the canvas of crystalline charm stay,
To guide our hearts through the frosty ballet.

Frosty Fleeting Moments

Each breath we take is a crystal so clear,
In frosty moments, our hearts draw near.
Timeless the peace that wraps us tight,
As winter descends, painting dreams with white.

A fleeting whisper, a chill on the cheek,
Reminds us of warmth that we all still seek.
Sunrise awakens, a soft, golden hue,
Kissing the frost, as the day starts anew.

In these moments, we pause and admire,
The beauty that glimmers, our spirits inspire.
Time drifts like snowflakes that fall from above,
Whirling through life, embracing the love.

Laughter rings out through the crisp, frosty air,
Chasing the shadows, without a single care.
In memories fleeting, like glimmers of light,
We find warmth together, igniting the night.

Frosty fleeting moments, so precious, so rare,
Wrap around us in a delicate flare.
Cherished forever, as seasons will turn,
In our hearts, the warmth of these moments will burn.

Echoes of a Still Heart

In silence, we listen to whispers of past,
Echoes of moments that fade all too fast.
A still heart remembers the love that once grew,
Filling the chambers with echoes of you.

Time gently brushes like leaves in the breeze,
A quiet reflection that brings us to ease.
Through shadows we wander, with hope in our gaze,
Seeking the light in the soft morning haze.

Each heartbeat a memory that dances inside,
Resonant whispers where secrets abide.
In stillness we find the strength to move on,
Embracing the echoes as night gives to dawn.

Yet shadows may flicker, and doubts may arise,
The still heart remains, where our courage lies.
With every soft pulse, the journey expands,
Uniting our spirits, entwined in life's hands.

From echoes of silence grows a serene art,
A tapestry woven within the still heart.
In this gentle space, where all can be whole,
We cherish the echoes that nourish the soul.

The Chill of Silent Nights

The moon hangs low in the sky,
Casting shadows on the ground.
Whispers dance in the cool air,
While the world wraps in a shroud.

Frosted breath escapes my lips,
As I wonder through the dark.
Stars like diamonds softly glint,
Leaving behind their silent mark.

A crackling fire waits for me,
But here, I seek the night's embrace.
Each sound a fleeting memory,
Each moment a tranquil space.

The chill wraps tightly around me,
While stillness claims the land.
Nature speaks in hushed tones,
In this frozen, tranquil strand.

Alone, yet never lonely,
The night brings peace to my soul.
In the chill of silent nights,
I find where I am whole.

Dreams Adorned in White

Softly, the snowflakes whisper,
Cloaking the world in pure white.
Every branch, each quiet rooftop,
Sparkles beneath the moonlight.

Children laugh in winter's grasp,
Building castles of frosty dreams.
In their eyes, the joy of life,
As they dance in snowy beams.

Footprints trace a delicate path,
Stories written on the ground.
Every step a wish ignites,
In this winter wonderland found.

Within the stillness of the night,
Silent wishes take their flight.
Wrapped in dreams adorned in white,
We drift gently into the light.

As dawn breaks, colors arise,
Merging with the pristine scene.
Though dreams may fade with daylight,
Their magic lingers in between.

Glacial Echoes

In the valleys, silence reigns,
Echoes ripple through the air.
Glacial whispers brush my skin,
Telling tales of winter's flair.

Icebergs drift on a sapphire sea,
Time frozen in a crystalline trance.
Each crack and creak, a lullaby,
Nature's rhythm, a heart's dance.

Steps taken on this ancient ice,
Where footsteps leave a fleeting trace.
Breath mingles with the chilling air,
In this haunting, sacred space.

Underneath the frigid stars,
Secrets of the earth reside.
Glacial echoes sing their song,
In the vastness, we confide.

As I wander through the night,
Heart open to the world's embrace.
These moments, fleeting yet profound,
Illuminate this frozen place.

Hushed Footsteps on Icy Paths

Hushed footsteps tread on icy paths,
The world encased in glimmering white.
Each crunch beneath feels like a prayer,
A whisper shared with the night.

Frozen branches bow with weight,
Marvels wrapped in nature's grace.
As the dawn begins its ascent,
I find solace in this place.

Clouds hang low, a gentle veil,
Softly cradling the breaking day.
Beneath the frost, life quietly breathes,
Waiting for the sun's warm ray.

Every step a moment cherished,
In the hush of the morning's glow.
Wonders unfold with every breath,
In the quiet beauty of snow.

With each icy path I wander,
I feel the world come alive.
Hushed footsteps lead me onward,
In this dance where dreams survive.

Dances in the Stillness

In silent woods where shadows play,
The leaves do twirl in soft ballet.
A breeze whispers secrets untold,
As time moves gently, calm and bold.

Moonlight drapes the earth so bright,
Guiding dreams into the night.
Stars twinkle high, a celestial guide,
While quiet moments dance beside.

The brook sings soft its lullaby,
While crickets chirp, they flutter by.
Nature holds its breath so fine,
In stillness, joy and peace align.

Closed eyes see the world anew,
Awake, we feel the night's cool dew.
In every corner, whispers play,
The heart beats softly, night turns day.

So let us roam through whispered air,
As magic swirls, beyond compare.
In stillness, beauty takes its place,
In every dance, the world we embrace.

Ephemeral Frosts

A crystal cloak on fields does lie,
Where winter's breath steals breaths nearby.
Each spark a promise, fleeting, bright,
In morning's glow, a world of light.

Footsteps crunch on frosty ground,
As whispers of the cold resound.
Nature weaves a tapestry,
Of fragile beauty, set so free.

The sun climbs slow, a golden crown,
Kissing frost, before it drowns.
Each moment fleeting, gone too fast,
Yet in their grace, forever cast.

Boughs bow low with jeweled tears,
A silent song for all our years.
In soft embrace, the cold does hold,
The tales of winter, pure and bold.

Yet as the day begins to fade,
The frost will thaw, the light cascade.
To memories, it bids adieu,
In every glance, a spark anew.

Arctic Murmurs

In lands where silence reigns supreme,
The icy winds begin to dream.
Beneath the auroras, colors glide,
A dance of lights where shadows hide.

Whispers echo through the night,
A lull of snow, a soft delight.
The moon reflects on frozen seas,
While winter holds its breath, at ease.

Pale glaciers creak in ancient song,
As time moves slow, yet never long.
In white embrace, the world feels still,
A tranquil pulse, a gentle thrill.

Each snowflake falls, a story new,
In tones of blue and silver hue.
The heart of winter beats so loud,
In icy realms, we stand so proud.

Listen closely, hear the sound,
Of nature's whispers all around.
In Arctic dreams, we find our way,
A world that stirs both night and day.

Shards of Crystal Light

In twilight's glow, the crystals spark,
Illuminating shadows dark.
As splinters dance on evening's breath,
They twirl with grace, defying death.

Each shard reflects a tale of old,
Of moments cherished, dreams retold.
In every glint, a story sings,
Of times we soared on fragile wings.

The light filters through branches bare,
Creating patterns, fine and rare.
Each flicker tells of hopes and fears,
A mosaic woven through the years.

When day gives way to starry night,
The shards of dreams ignite with light.
In every heartbeat, every sigh,
We find the whispers that draw nigh.

So let us gather, hearts aligned,
And seek the beauty life can bind.
In crystal shards, we find our place,
And share the warmth of love's embrace.

A Palette of Icy Dreams

In the pale glow of the moonlight,
Colors blend, a spectral sight.
Whispers of frost on winter's breath,
Drawing paintings, life and death.

Snowflakes dance, a silent song,
Each shard of ice, where dreams belong.
With every hue, a story told,
In this world, both bright and cold.

Through glistening trees, shadows play,
As winter's veil sweeps night to day.
A canvas bright with nature's grace,
Where time stands still in this embrace.

Reflections shimmer on frozen streams,
Echoing softly, our heart's dreams.
A palette rich with icy gleams,
Creating whispers of lost themes.

As dawn breaks forth, the colors fade,
Yet memories linger, never strayed.
In the twilight, a soft reprise,
Of icy dreams beneath the skies.

The Magic Wand of Frost

Waves of silver, softly glide,
The magic wand casts wide aside.
Blankets of snow, patches of white,
Transforming day into quiet night.

A twinkle dances in frosty air,
Each flake a charm, beyond compare.
With gentle touch, old worlds reborn,
In winter's arms, the earth is sworn.

Wondrous spells spun from the chill,
Nature reinforces, bends to will.
Trees adorned, a sparkling gown,
Majestic beauty all around.

With every breath, the chill reveals,
A world where magic softly heals.
As stardust rains from skies so vast,
In frosty nights, the die is cast.

We chase the shadows and leave our trace,
In whispered secrets, we find our place.
With the wand of frost, dreams align,
In winter's heart, our souls entwine.

Serenity Wrapped in Cold

In twilight's grasp, the quiet reigns,
A world asleep, beneath the chains.
Blankets soft, of white and gray,
Our worries lost, at close of day.

The silence hums a soothing sound,
Where every flake falls to the ground.
Wrapped in cold, the heart finds peace,
As winter whispers, all must cease.

Footsteps crunch on frosted paths,
Nature beams with gentle laughs.
Each breath a cloud in frosty air,
In frozen stillness, life laid bare.

Peaceful moments, time stands still,
Flowing softly, as dreams fulfill.
Serenity sings in every fold,
Wrapped in warmth, though days be cold.

As stars awaken, shining bright,
The world ignites with sheer delight.
In icy grip, our spirits soar,
For in the cold, we find so much more.

Frosted Portraits of Time

In the gallery of frosted hues,
Life's moments freeze, like morning dew.
Framed in ice, each tale unfolds,
A story whispered, vibrant and bold.

Captured smiles in glistening frames,
Echoes of laughter, flickering flames.
Frosty portraits, memories dear,
Frozen in time, forever near.

With every glance, a past unveiled,
In silver glows, the heart's impaled.
Moments cherished, never lost,
In winter's chill, we count the cost.

As seasons shift and moments pass,
The frosted frames will still amass.
Through icy lenses, we see the light,
In portraits of time, dark turns bright.

The gallery stands in silent grace,
With every glance, a sweet embrace.
Frosted tales of laughter and pain,
In time's portrait, we find and remain.

When the World Slumbers

When night drapes its quiet cloak,
The stars whisper secrets so soft.
In shadows where moonlight glows,
Dreams awaken, gently aloft.

The world holds its breath in peace,
As silence weaves a soothing sound.
Time pauses, granting release,
In this refuge, solace is found.

Beneath the slumbering skies,
Hope takes flight on silver wings.
In the darkness, the heart sighs,
For joy in twilight gently clings.

Every flicker and twinkle's kiss,
Encapsulates the essence of night.
Wrapped in a shroud of bliss,
We dwell in dreams, pure and bright.

When the world rests and sighs,
In the cradle of sleep, we stay.
With each heartbeat, love complies,
As dawn awaits to light the way.

The Magic of Crystallized Moments

In the pause of a fleeting glance,
Time freezes, sparkling like dew.
Each second a shimmering dance,
Magic unfolds, radiant and new.

Memories caught in icy frames,
Whisper stories of days gone by.
Like diamonds, they hold our names,
In the heart, they never die.

With laughter echoing through air,
These moments, a treasure, they weave.
Wrapped in a love, pure and rare,
In memory's arms, we believe.

The chill of the night gently stirs,
As stars blink, their secrets to share.
In each memory, the heart purrs,
For magic resides everywhere.

Crystallized in our minds like glass,
Every sparkle, a tale to tell.
In the embrace of time, they pass,
Yet in our souls, they always dwell.

A Gallery of Glistening Dreams

In the hush of twilight's glow,
Dreams emerge like stars above.
Each one, a brushstroke's flow,
In this gallery, we find love.

Across the canvas of the night,
Glistening visions twirl and play.
In colors bold, they take flight,
Painting hope in a magical way.

As the moonlight drapes its veil,
Wishes hang like lanterns high.
Every heartbeat tells a tale,
In the dreamscape, we learn to fly.

The whispers of hope entwine,
With every shimmer, every gleam.
In this dance, we redefine,
The boundaries of what we dream.

Here in this gallery of light,
Infinite journeys await our stride.
With courage, we chase the night,
In dreams, we're forever allied.

Secrets Carved in Ice

In the depths of winter's chill,
Secrets whisper, soft as snow.
Each flake, a story to fulfill,
As frozen winds begin to blow.

Through crystalline corridors,
Echoes of laughter gently glide.
Encased in the frost, they're ours,
In icy realms, we safely bide.

The silence speaks in shimmering tones,
With every crack, a world unfolds.
In the stillness, the heart atones,
For dreams that time bravely holds.

Within the frost, memories gleam,
Like jewels cast upon a stream.
In every shard, a forgotten dream,
Where hopes linger, thin and supreme.

Secrets carved in nature's art,
In fleeting moments, life takes flight.
Through the chill, we guard our heart,
For in the cold, warmth sparks light.

The Peace of Winter's Breath

Snowflakes dance upon the air,
Whispers soft, a gentle prayer.
Trees adorned in coats of white,
Silent eve, the world feels right.

Fires crackle, warmth inside,
Hushed moments, hearts abide.
The moon hangs low, a silver thread,
Guiding dreams where peace is spread.

Children laugh, their voices cheer,
In frosty fields, they draw near.
Time slows down, worries cease,
In this realm, we find our peace.

Icicles gleam in morning light,
Nature's gems, a pure delight.
The cold air sharp, yet soothing too,
Winter's breath, a tranquil view.

As twilight falls, the stars ignite,
A canvas of dreams, soft and bright.
In the hush of winter's grace,
We find solace, our sacred space.

Hibernation Haven

In the heart of winter's glow,
Creatures seek their warmth below.
Burrows deep, where dreams inscribe,
Nature's pause, a quiet vibe.

Soft blankets of moss weave tight,
Cradling life in cozy night.
The world above, a frozen tale,
Beneath the snow, the brave prevail.

Seeds lie still, in slumber deep,
Awaiting spring, their dreams to leap.
In still waters, reflections wait,
Time flows slow, in gentle fate.

Stars blink down from velvet skies,
As night whispers its lullabies.
The moon guards all, a watchful eye,
In hibernation, moments sigh.

With every breath, the silence hums,
In nature's rest, a promise comes.
When warmth returns, the world will thrive,
For now, we're still, and so alive.

The Allure of Soft Crystals

Glistening gems beneath the sky,
Each flake a wonder, pure and spry.
Nature's art, a frozen lace,
Whispers of winter's sweet embrace.

Delicate forms, a fleeting sight,
Sparkling softly in the night.
Each one a tale, unique, divine,
Captured moments, frozen time.

Children spin to catch the fall,
Dancing lightly, heed the call.
A world transformed where dreams take flight,
In the allure of soft moonlight.

These crystal wonders fade away,
Yet memories in hearts will stay.
A fleeting joy, a brief romance,
In winter's magic, we find our chance.

So let us cherish every drift,
The gentle dance, the quiet gift.
For in their glow, true beauty lies,
Soft crystals paint the snowy skies.

Glacial Gardens in Twilight

Where ice and dusk begin to blend,
A garden blooms that will transcend.
Glacial petals, shimmer and gleam,
In twilight's glow, they dance and dream.

Frigid blooms in shades of blue,
Kissed by stars, the night's debut.
Whispers cool as shadows creep,
In nature's heart, a secret keep.

Each frozen branch a work of art,
Nature's beauty, close to heart.
Underneath a veil of night,
The glacial gardens shimmer bright.

The air is crisp, a breath of peace,
In winter's grasp, our cares release.
As silence falls, the world holds breath,
In twilight's arms, we find our depth.

So wander through this icy land,
A tranquil peace, a gentle hand.
In glacial gardens, dreams will weave,
A winter's night, a heart's reprieve.

Lapland Lullabies

Whispers of snowflakes drift down,
Softly they dance in a silvery gown.
Stars twinkle bright in the deep night sky,
Nature sings sweetly, a lullaby sigh.

Moonlight kisses the frozen ground,
In this still world, peace is found.
Dreams weave like threads in the cold air,
Gentle embrace, a soothing prayer.

Pine trees stand tall, cloaked in white,
Guardians of secrets whispered at night.
Frosted branches cradle the dreams,
Under the glow of the starlit beams.

Children's laughter, echoes of glee,
Chasing the snow that dips from the tree.
Lapland's charm, a magical tune,
Cradled in arms of a shimmering moon.

As the world wraps in a soft dark shroud,
Whispers are heard, gentle and loud.
In this land where silence holds sway,
Lapland's lullabies guide the way.

Embracing Frosted Silence

Upon the canvas of winter's breath,
Frosted silence dances, life and death.
Nature's stillness, a moment divine,
In the hush of the snow, we entwine.

Each crystal flake tells a tale untold,
In the layered silence, secrets unfold.
Branches heavy with a silky sheen,
Whispering softly, serene and keen.

Footsteps quiet, muffled in white,
Embracing the calm of the frosted night.
Winds weave softly through ancient trees,
Melodies carried on a breath of freeze.

In this frozen embrace, time seems to pause,
Capturing moments for hearts to appraise.
Glimmers of hope in the shadows ahead,
In the warmth of silence, nothing's left unsaid.

Stars blink like gems in a velvet expanse,
As dreams swirl softly, lost in a trance.
Frosted silence, both cradle and shield,
Within its embrace, our spirits are healed.

The Tenderness of Cold

Chill in the air, a gentle caress,
Embracing us softly, a tender impress.
Frost on the branches, dogwood and pine,
Whispers of winter, a delicate sign.

Each breath a cloud in the icy night,
Moments of stillness wrapped in white light.
Stars cast reflections, from heavens above,
Illuminating the world in a tender love.

Under the blanket of winter's embrace,
We find our solace, our sacred space.
The world slows down, heartbeats align,
In the tenderness of cold, we intertwine.

As daylight fades, shadows stretch long,
Nature hums softly, a gentle song.
In the silence of dusk, we gather our peace,
From the tenderness of cold, we find release.

Embers glow softly in the hearth's warm light,
As we find shelter from the coming night.
Wrapped in the stillness, the world feels whole,
In winter's embrace, we nourish the soul.

Shadows of the Celestial Night

Beneath the heavens, where starlight flows,
Shadows of nightguard the world below.
Moonbeams dance lightly on dew-kissed grass,
In the quiet of darkness, moments shall pass.

The vast cosmos whispers in silvery tones,
Stories of ages, of gods, and of bones.
Each twinkle a memory, lost yet profound,
In shadows of night, mysteries abound.

Clouds drift like dreams over slumbering hills,
Restless and roving, these nightborne thrills.
Tales of creation, of light born from dark,
Nestled in shadows, a deep-hidden spark.

As night paints the sky with its velvet cloak,
The universe breathes, a celestial joke.
Stars wane and flicker, a cosmic ballet,
Guiding our spirits as we find our way.

In the shadows of night, we gather our thoughts,
Floating through galaxies, time is distraught.
In silence we wander, both lost and found,
In shadows of celestial night, we're unbound.

Sapphire Skies

Beneath the expanse, a canvas so blue,
Whispers of dreams in the breezes that blew.
Clouds drifting softly like thoughts in our mind,
Sapphire skies hold the secrets we find.

Sunlight will dance on the edges of day,
Casting long shadows where children will play.
Awakening hearts in the warmth of the light,
Sapphire skies promise a future so bright.

A hint of the evening begins to unfold,
As stars start to twinkle, their stories retold.
Moonbeams will weave through the fabric of night,
In sapphire skies wrapped in soft, gentle light.

Each moment cherished, each breath that we take,
With nature embracing, our spirits awake.
In harmony's grasp, we rise and we soar,
Sapphire skies cradle forevermore.

So let us rejoice in this beautiful hue,
Where dreams weave themselves in the vastness so true.
With hope as our compass, we'll find our way home,
Under sapphire skies, we are never alone.

Icy Ground

Upon the earth, a glistening sheet,
The icy ground whispers beneath our feet.
With every step, a crackling sound,
Nature's beauty wrapped in frost all around.

Silvery crystals in the morning light,
Glistening diamonds, a wondrous sight.
Nature wears cloaks of winter's embrace,
As we explore this enchanting place.

Frozen branches reach to the sky,
In icy silence, time seems to fly.
Footprints linger where warmth once resides,
In the heart of winter, beauty abides.

The world is a canvas painted in white,
Under cold skies, everything feels right.
Harmonious stillness, as night takes its reign,
The icy ground whispers, a soft, sweet refrain.

Embrace the chill, let the cold air flow,
For in icy silence, our spirits will grow.
A moment of peace in a world so profound,
Together we'll dance on the icy ground.

Enchantment of the Snowbound

In a realm where the snowflakes gently fall,
Whispers of magic enchant one and all.
Each flake a story, unique and divine,
In the enchantment of snowbound, we find.

Blanketing earth in a shimmering hue,
The world transforms into something anew.
Each branch adorned in a frosty display,
In the stillness of night, dreams come out to play.

Footsteps echo through a wintery spell,
Where secrets of nature in silence dwell.
Glistening landscapes that sparkle and gleam,
In the enchantment of snowbound, we dream.

With laughter that dances on chilled winter air,
Moments together, a warmth we can share.
Hot cocoa steaming, our hearts intertwined,
In this sanctuary, peace is defined.

As twilight descends and the stars brightly glow,
We cherish the bliss that this season bestows.
In the magic of snow, forever be bound,
In the enchantment of winter, love can be found.

Secrets in the Snowdrift

Amidst the silence, the secrets unfold,
In snowdrifts hidden, stories untold.
Footprints converge in a delicate dance,
Whispers of winter ignite a sweet chance.

Beneath the layers where shadows do hide,
Nature provides where mysteries bide.
Each crystal glittering, a tale to share,
In secrets of snowdrifts, we breathe the cold air.

Glimmers of laughter, the warmth of a fire,
Our hearts intertwine with a shared desire.
As winter envelops our dreams in bright white,
The secrets in snowdrifts illuminate night.

Frost-kissed moments, where time stands still,
The beauty surrounds us, an unspoken thrill.
Together we weave through this world side by side,
Finding our solace in secrets that glide.

So come take a journey, let wonders arise,
In the land of the snowdrift, beneath open skies.
With hearts open wide, let our spirits take flight,
These secrets of winter will guide us tonight.

Frost-Kissed Serenade

In gardens where silence drapes its white veil,
A frost-kissed serenade sings soft as the gale.
Branches embrace the weight of the snow,
In this tranquil beauty, our spirits will grow.

The air bites gently, a crisp winter tune,
Under the silver gaze of a midday moon.
Each note, a whisper that dances on air,
In a frost-kissed serenade, dreams galore share.

Gather around where warmth will ignite,
With laughter and stories that sparkle so bright.
Hot chocolate warming our hands close in tight,
Frost-kissed serenade serenades the night.

Nature's soft hymn plays as daylight will fade,
With stars overhead, the night serenade.
Each breath that we take melts worry and fear,
In this frost-kissed embrace, love will draw near.

So let us rejoice, let our voices unite,
In a symphony crafted by joy and delight.
In the heart of winter, together we'll sing,
Frost-kissed serenade, our spirits take wing.

The Art of Frost

Upon the glass, a crystal grid,
Nature's breath; a silent bid.
Delicate patterns, fleeting grace,
A whispered touch, a frozen lace.

Morning light, it softly gleams,
Turning frost to silver dreams.
A painter's brush on winter's own,
In chilly air, artistry grown.

Every flake, a world designed,
In icy realms, our hearts aligned.
Each sculpture speaks of time in pause,
Nature's pause, a frozen cause.

As sunlight breaks the chilly night,
Frost gives way to warmth and light.
Yet in the heart, a memory stays,
Of winter's breath in woven ways.

In this art of frost we find,
A truth profound, a bond defined.
Through icy paths, our spirits roam,
In fleeting beauty, we feel home.

Frosty Photographs

Captured moments, frozen bright,
Frosty scenes in morning light.
Each picture tells a tale untold,
A silent whisper, brave and bold.

Branches draped in icy chains,
Nature's canvas, pure refrains.
Framed in crystal, time stands still,
Memory held in winter's chill.

Children's laughter, snowflakes dance,
Frolicking in a playful trance.
Snapshots bright, a treasured gaze,
Frosty magic, in childhood's maze.

Fields of white, a quilt of grace,
Every scene a warm embrace.
Through lens we see, through heart we feel,
Frozen moments become real.

In the stillness, beauty flows,
Frosty photographs, a gentle prose.
Every click, a story spun,
Within the frost, our lives run.

A Tapestry of Frozen Hues

Threads of blue in winter's weave,
A tapestry, we dare believe.
Shades of white, a silken drift,
Of frozen hues, nature's gift.

Silver glimmers, ice's art,
Crafted softly, nature's heart.
Glimpses catching morning's rise,
A dance of colors 'neath the skies.

Crisp and cool, the air imbues,
Every breath, a painting of views.
Frozen rivers twinkle bright,
Embroidered dreams, the world alight.

Underneath the frost, we dwell,
In frozen shades, a tale to tell.
Nature's fingers deftly trace,
A woven world, a still embrace.

In twilight hues, our spirits lift,
This frozen tapestry, a gift.
Through each layer, life prevails,
In winter's art, our heart unveils.

A Hearth's Warmth Under Starlight

Under stars, the night does glow,
A hearth's warmth, a gentle flow.
Crackling flames, we gather near,
In whispered tales, we find our cheer.

Outside, the frost, a silver sheet,
While inside, hearts dance with heat.
Laughter mingles with the night,
Together lost in pure delight.

Shadows flicker, stories weave,
In the warmth, we dare believe.
While frost may cover the world wide,
In this glow, our hearts abide.

Underneath the cosmic dome,
This hearth's warmth feels like home.
As stars twinkle in skies so bright,
We cherish each soft, fleeting light.

In the stillness, love ignites,
Beneath the stars, our souls take flight.
A hearth's embrace, where spirits blend,
In winter's chill, warmth never ends.

The Secrets in the Snowfall

Whispers dance upon the ground,
As flakes drift softly, unbound.
Each one holds a tale untold,
In winter's arms, the secrets unfold.

Footprints fade in the white embrace,
Moonlight mingles in silent grace.
Nature's hush, a world asleep,
In snow's embrace, the secrets keep.

Glistening dreams in frosty air,
Woven magic everywhere.
A shiver runs, a spirit flies,
In every flake, a piece of skies.

Frosted edges frame the scene,
Where laughter lingers, pure and keen.
Children play in drifting white,
Chasing shadows, hearts take flight.

Beneath the still, the heart will sigh,
In every flake, a gentle cry.
The stories told in glistening hues,
Of winter's grace, and soft goodbyes.

The Sublime Silence of Chill

In the quiet of the evening glow,
A breath of wind begins to flow.
Chill descends with a gentle hand,
Wrapping the earth in a silken band.

Winter whispers secrets true,
In the hush, the moon shines through.
Stars blink softly in the night,
Wrapped in shadows, bathed in light.

The air is crisp, a perfect freeze,
As trees stand tall with graceful ease.
Silence reigns, a calm delight,
In the sublime glow of starry night.

Frosty breath on windowpanes,
A canvas where stillness reigns.
Time stands still, a moment's bliss,
In the chill, the world we kiss.

Wrapped in warmth, we sip our tea,
Embracing the cold serenity.
The world outside feels far away,
In the sublime silence, we wish to stay.

Stillness in a Frosted Veil

Veils of frost on nature's face,
Whispers echo, a sacred space.
Everything sleeps in quiet grace,
In winter's arms, dreams interlace.

Softly falls the glistening light,
Weightless flakes in the fading night.
A gentle sigh upon the ground,
In stillness, magic can be found.

Branches bow with silver threads,
Hushed the world as twilight spreads.
In the frosted veil we wander,
Where fleeting moments make us ponder.

Each breath visible, crisp and clear,
In the hush, the heart draws near.
Nature's beauty, soft and stark,
Illuminates the world in dark.

Stillness woven through the trees,
Whistling winds like distant seas.
Caught in a dream, so calm and frail,
We find our peace in the frosted veil.

Frost-kissed Memories

Memories linger on icy trails,
In every flake, a story hails.
Footprints etched in the winter's breath,
Marking moments, alive in death.

Frozen laughter fills the night,
Echoes of joy, pure and bright.
In frosty air, the past resides,
In every gust, the heart confides.

Time slips softly, like falling snow,
Holding hands in the twilight glow.
Every glimmer, a cherished face,
In frost-kissed memories, we find our place.

Warmth of stories, softly told,
In winter's embrace, we gather gold.
The chill may bite, but hearts stay warm,
In memories forged through love's sweet charm.

As seasons shift and moments fade,
The frost remains, the memories made.
In every flake that touches the ground,
Frost-kissed echoes forever sound.

Cascades of Icy Wonder

Glistening streams of icy flow,
Whispers of winter softly blow.
Crystal droplets dance and twirl,
Nature's art in a chilly whirl.

Mountains draped in blanket white,
Silent echoes of pure delight.
Frozen landscapes gleam and shine,
Magic woven in each line.

Rivers sleep beneath the frost,
Beauty gained and beauty lost.
Snowflakes kiss the silent ground,
In their fall, sweet peace is found.

Trees adorned with silver lace,
Cascades weave a wondrous grace.
Each branch holds a sparkling dream,
Where the world stands still, it seems.

A hush befalls the starry night,
In the stillness, hearts feel right.
Cascades of wonder, cold and bright,
Whispers of magic in the light.

Shadows beneath the Frosted Moon

Silent night with shadows cast,
Underneath the moonlight's blast.
Frosty whispers weave through trees,
Carried softly by the breeze.

Ghosts of winter trace the glade,
In their dance, a cool parade.
Stars sparkling like icy fire,
Hearts ignited with desire.

Pale moonlight on the frozen lake,
Dreams unfold and softly wake.
Shadows shift with eerie grace,
As if hiding a secret place.

Beneath the frost, a world lies still,
Nature sleeps, the night's goodwill.
Whispers of old tales retold,
In the silence, stories unfold.

Time stands still, a magic loom,
Weaving dreams 'neath the frosted moon.
In this moment, all feels clear,
Winter's beauty drawing near.

Entranced by the Bitter Chill

A breath of wind, a burst of cold,
Nature's charms begin to unfold.
Entranced by the winter's grasp,
In her beauty, we tightly clasp.

The bite of frost upon the air,
A crisp invitation, bold and rare.
Footsteps crunch on blankets deep,
As the world lies calm, and we keep.

Fires crackle with warmth so bright,
Chasing shadows from the night.
Cocoa sipped by candlelight,
Entranced in magic, hearts take flight.

The stars awaken, bold above,
In the chill, we find our love.
Each frosty spark, a gleaming thrill,
Together lost in the bitter chill.

Embrace the night, let worries cease,
In winter's arms, we find our peace.
With every shiver, joy we instill,
In this season, we feel the thrill.

The Comfort of Winter Fires

Flickering flames in a cozy nook,
Stories shared in a warming book.
Laughter dances with the light,
In the heart of a chilly night.

Smoke rises in a gentle swirl,
A soft embrace, our hearts unfurl.
Mittens warm and blankets tight,
Together bound, we feel the light.

Outside, the snowflakes fall and sigh,
While inside, warmth draws us nigh.
Every crackle tells a tale,
Of winter's magic, crisp and frail.

The glow of embers, soft and low,
Such sweet comfort in the flow.
Seasons change, yet still we stay,
Wrapped in warmth while cold holds sway.

In the hearth, love finds its spark,
Against the chill, we make our mark.
Fires will burn, and hearts desire,
The comfort found in winter's fire.

Milton Keynes UK
Ingram Content Group UK Ltd.
UKHW010231111224
452348UK00011B/684